THE VANISHING DEPOT

THE VANISHING DEPOT

Ranulph Bye, A.W.S.

LIVINGSTON PUBLISHING COMPANY
Wynnewood, Pennsylvania

Library of Congress Cataloging in Publication Data

Bye, Ranulph, 1916—
  The vanishing depot.

  1. Bye, Ranulph, 1916— 2. Railroads—United
States—Stations—Pictorial works. I. Title.
ND1839.B93A57   759.13   73-16229
ISBN 0-87098-058-0

To The Memory of My Father

ARTHUR EDWIN BYE

Artist, Author, Historian

Contents

Foreword	xi	Overbrook, Philadelphia, Pennsylvania	49
Preface	xiii	Fairmount Park, Philadelphia, Pennsylvania	50
Introduction	1	Upsal, Philadelphia, Pennsylvania	51
Wilkes-Barre, Pennsylvania	6, 7	Wissahickon, Philadelphia, Pennsylvania	52
Bloomsburg, Pennsylvania	9	Allen Lane, Philadelphia, Pennsylvania	53
Jim Thorpe, Pennsylvania	11	Wayne, Pennsylvania	54
Northumberland, Pennsylvania	12	Bryn Mawr, Pennsylvania	55
Easton, Pennsylvania	13, 14, 15	Strafford, Pennsylvania	57
Bethlehem, Pennsylvania	17	North Wales, Pennsylvania	58
Allentown, Pennsylvania	19, 20, 21, 22, 23	Mt. Airy, Pennsylvania	59
Topton, Pennsylvania	24	New Britain, Pennsylvania	60
Reinholds, Pennsylvania	25	Sellersville, Pennsylvania	61
Birdsboro, Pennsylvania	26	Doylestown, Pennsylvania	62
Sinking Spring, Pennsylvania	27	Perkasie, Pennsylvania	63
Lebanon, Pennsylvania	29	Wycombe, Pennsylvania	65
Gettysburg, Pennsylvania	31	New Hope, Pennsylvania	66, 67
Point of Rocks, Maryland	32	Lambertville, New Jersey	68, 69
York, Pennsylvania	33	Hopewell, New Jersey	70, 71
Ellicott City, Maryland	35	Pennington, New Jersey	72
Laurel, Maryland	36	Skillman, New Jersey	73
Takoma, Maryland	37	Manville-Finderne, New Jersey	74
Rockville, Maryland	38	Weston-Manville, New Jersey	75
Gaithersburg, Maryland	39	Milford, New Jersey	76
Harpers Ferry, West Virginia	41	Elizabeth, New Jersey	77
Clayton, Delaware	42	Fanwood, New Jersey	78, 79
Hammonton, New Jersey	43	Jersey City, New Jersey	80, 81
Mt. Holly, New Jersey	44	Hackensack, New Jersey	82
Chatsworth, New Jersey	45	Lyndhurst, New Jersey	83
Cossart, Pennsylvania	47	Great Meadows, New Jersey	84, 85
Glen Mills, Pennsylvania	48	Tenafly, New Jersey	86, 87

Demarest, New Jersey   88   Waterbury, Connecticut   99

Hillsdale, New Jersey   89   Thomaston, Connecticut   100

Bronx, New York   90   Cos Cob, Connecticut   101

Sparkill, New York   91   Peacedale, Rhode Island   103

Peekskill, New York   92   Buzzards Bay, Massachusetts   105

Kingston, New York   93   Chatham, Massachusetts   107

Wurtsboro, New York   94   Whitman, Massachusetts   108, 109

Old Saybrook, Connecticut   95   Middlebury, Vermont   110

Stamford, Connecticut   97   Crawford Notch, New Hampshire   111

Cannan, Connecticut   98   North Conway, New Hampshire   113

Where is the bustle and chatter
  The sound of the clanging gates?
The clock that a gentleman hurries
  As a loved one he awaits?

Where are the redcaps and porters,
  The engineer, King of the Day?
Like a mist falling over the ocean
  Their image is fading away.

This depot was once lord of Main Street
  The Victorian master of town
Now the windows and shutters are broken
  Its torn roof is sagging down.

What wonderful memories it harbors
  The echoes of laughter and tears
Like a scene from the past in a daydream
  The depot disappears.

Rita Loftus Gross

Foreword

In the early days of railroading, the local depot was a source of community pride. As time passed, it generally was taken for granted, a hardly-noticed town fixture. Only recently has it, once again, come into focus, since the curtailment of passenger services has signalled the end of many a landmark.

Railroadiana always had many enthusiasts, because of the historical importance of locomotives and rolling stock. With the cutback in passenger service, many more have joined the ranks of railroad buffs, looking back with nostalgia at this significant part of Americana.

The sudden boom in railroad interest carried over to the stations. In this volume, Mr. Bye's talents help perpetuate these structures for us, and rekindle memories of railroading in its heyday. He has painted these buildings of that bygone era and given each a lasting measure of pride. I know that as you look at each painting, you will agree.

EDWIN P. ALEXANDER

Preface

This book is an attempt to illustrate some of the unique stations I have
come across in my travels up and down the east coast during the past
12 years. All the stations depicted here in watercolor were painted on
location or from pictures taken on the spot. It is regrettable that many
have been razed since this project began. Since most of the more
interesting stations were built during the early days of railroading over
a century ago, I am limiting this study to depots built prior to 1900
except, in rare cases, where I found a few of particular interest built
since that period. Included here are also freight stations, signal towers,
watchman's shanties and some architectural details of stations. To keep
the book in its historical context the identification of stations is related
to the railroads which they originally served, and not necessarily the
present operating company.

I express appreciation to the following institutions which have kindly
given permission to have their works reproduced: The Smithsonian
Institution (National Museum of History and Technology) and the
William Penn Museum of the Pennsylvania Historical and Museum
Commission in Harrisburg. Also to Edwin P. Alexander for making
available his research material, and to the American Heritage Publishing
Company for the information it provided.

Many people were kind enough to answer my letters of inquiry,
return my phone calls, and volunteer to dig through records to help
me research this book. George Hart of the Pennsylvania Historical and
Museum Commission, W. C. Humphreys, and Al Chamberlain of Penn
Central Railroad, Edgar A. Riddle of the Lehigh Valley Railroad, Harry
P. Albrecht, Publisher *Steam Locomotives of Yesteryear,* James M.
Bourne, of the Baltimore and Ohio Railroad, Lois Morasco, W. H. Kiehl,
The Chessie System, Nathan James, and George W. Eastland are a few
of these people, and to those others inadvertantly omitted, my sincere
thanks.

I also wish to express my gratitude to my friend and colleague, Bill
Loos, whose creative endeavor designed this book.

Introduction

This is a nostalgic journey into the golden age of railroading, the wondrous years that ended in the 1920's. The great iron horse was king of the road, well into its second century, but still full of steam and rarin' to go. But youthful contenders loomed large on the horizon, ready to take their places in transport history, the automobile, the airplane. Yet they, and no other means of transportation, ever achieved the personality of the old passenger train; and neither garage nor airport fell heir to the character and fascination of the rural depot.

Railroading had a resurgence or two after the 20's, serving our country well in the movement of men and material during the war years. But the trend which began in 1929 continued. Diminishing fares brought deficits to the lines with the consequent curtailment of passenger service and the demise of many country stations.

The depot was the hub of hamlet and town for 125 years. Not only was it the center of transportation, but the main source of communication and the symbol of the high road to adventure and opportunity. Lucius Beebe said that no other single structure or edifice has occupied as compelling a place in American consciousness as the railroad depot.

While Europe had already constructed magnificent terminals by 1865, the United States had mostly poorly-planned and makeshift buildings which were often constructed of wood that could be expected to go up in smoke at the first spark. By the 70's and 80's we were at least trying to compete, but the result was more often quaint, rather than magnificent. For the most part, the terminals reflected the individual architectural tastes of the wealthy owners of this booming industry.

In an attempt to imitate styles from abroad Americans were fond of using towers of some sort, preferably the picturesque feathers of Norman, Italian, Rhenish castle or some other unlikely design. Stations built from 1875 on were house-like structures incorporating all the architectural gimcracks of the period. The Queen Anne style was represented by a massive conical tower such as was used in Easton and Mauch Chunk (now Jim Thorpe, Pennsylvania). Sometimes a large cupola would set it apart from the ordinary. Most stations located in built-up areas had accommodations for the agents and their families who lived upstairs. The smaller depots on back country spurs were simple affairs containing only a waiting room and ticket office, and perhaps a separate room for baggage. They often resembled fancy gate houses of large estates found in the suburbs of big cities. The most distinguishing feature of the American depot was the copious overhanging roof which usually skirted the entire building to give protection for passengers on the platforms and entranceways. It is the hallmark of the "Railroad Style." As passenger service increased, even the platforms themselves were covered with a roof for 200 feet or more.

In New England, New Jersey, Pennsylvania and elsewhere, a gabled roof was simply extended in a straight line from the peak to 9 or 12 feet beyond the side of the building. In the case of two-story buildings, the overhang was supported by use of immense brackets. In stone or brick buildings these brackets were held in place by stone notches which extended a few inches from the outside wall.

The mansard roof was frequently used during the short era prior to 1876 and was commonly known as "General Grant Style", although this is a rather loose designation which took in everything with a mansard roof. Excellent examples of this style can be found in Bethlehem Pennsylvania, Hopewell and Pennington, New Jersey.

Throughout the 1850's, the railroads serving such cities as Philadelphia, New York, Harrisburg and Baltimore erected a number of substantial stations, and this trend became well established for years. Comparatively few smaller stations were architecturally designed. Generally most were planned by the railroads' engineering departments, built under their supervision by their carpenters and engineers. Stations by the hundreds, even thousands, were just utilitarian buildings. Fortunately, many others were distinctive in some form or other and these are the ones we remember for their picturesque quality.

Today the local railroad station is vanishing from the rural American scene almost as fast as the vanishing passenger train. And one can never be sure whether that one-story building standing forlornly where the depot used to be will house a lumber yard, office or a boutique.

The alert motorist who frequents the byways, rather than the turnpikes, can add to his touring enjoyment by making a game of searching out and identifying present and past railroad stations. This is not always easy, because the gables and scrollwork that were part of the late 19th-century architecture are rapidly disappearing behind advertising signs. In many cases all that is left is a bare spot on the ground where a station once stood, with only a broken cement platform left as a reminder. Stations on the Erie Lackawanna also are following the inevitable. For example, the building at Mountain Lakes, New Jersey is now a firehouse. Among the entires on the Delaware & Hudson's right of way are a firehouse, a shopping center and a discount store. And so it goes.

There are only a few stations still functioning today as they did during the heyday of American railroading, thanks to the resurgence of interest by railroad buffs. The New Hope, Pennsylvania depot is still in its original condition in spite of having been moved twice. Also in their original conditions are stations at Kempton and Strasburg, Pennsylvania, Middletown, New York, Hopewell, New Jersey and a beautiful one in Chester, Vermont.

Numbers of stations have been restored, such as the Fanwood, New Jersey and Bethlehem, Pennsylvania depots, by the Junior Chamber of Commerce, but these are no longer in service by the railroad. Suburban stations are still in use around metropolitan centers of the country for the convenience of commuters. But, for the most part, the rural station is now a memory of the past and the few that are left standing are boarded up or have been converted into a more profitable enterprise.

Says John Maas in *The Gingerbread Age:* "Today the railroad station is often a backwater on the wrong side of town. In the nineteenth century it was the hub of the community, the link to the Great World—the wretched roads were blocked by snow and mud for months, good highways came only after the automobile. Railroading was the nineteenth century's premier industry. It offered the finest careers to ambitious men, the most jobs to skilled workers. The Victorian railroad depot was a place of glamour and excitement and designed to look the part."

THE VANISHING DEPOT

Collection of John A. Meyer, Jr., Coach Inn, Ft. Washington, Pa.

WILKES-BARRE, PENNSYLVANIA

This Wilkes-Barre depot was built in 1870 as part of the Lehigh Valley Railroad System. It had two stories, but the main feature was its irregularly-shaped brick construction. It was sold with its surrounding land in 1963 and was later demolished.

WILKES-BARRE, PENNSYLVANIA

Patterned, perhaps, after a Victorian dovecote and built in 1868, this many-gabled structure is now a roost for commuting pigeons. Located on East Market Street, it was built to replace the former station near River Common, and was considered a model of its time. It was part of the Central Railroad of New Jersey on the main line between Wilkes-Barre and Jersey City. Passenger service was discontinued in 1963, and the station is now abandoned, threatened with demolition.

BLOOMSBURG, PENNSYLVANIA

Built in 1908, the watchman's shanty at
Bloomsburg is an example of the kind of
tiny building that was once common
throughout this country. It gave warmth
and cover to the crossing attendant in
inclement weather.

It was sold in 1966 and is now part of
a railroad museum.

JIM THORPE, PENNSYLVANIA

The town of Jim Thorpe, formerly known as Mauch Chunk, and renamed to honor the legendary Indian athlete, is located about 40 miles south of Wilkes-Barre. Its brick, two-story station with steeple-type roof is a counterpart of the one at Easton. The depot was built in 1888 and at one time accommodated literally hundreds of excursion trains in a season. It was also the commercial outlet of anthracite to Philadelphia and New York markets, and the home of millionaires associated with the flourishing coal industry.

Serviced by the Central Railroad of New Jersey prior to April of 1971, the Jim Thorpe station is now part of the Lehigh Valley Railroad; the station itself is unoccupied.

Ranulph Bye

11

NORTHUMBERLAND, PENNSYLVANIA

The brick station at Northumberland is located in scenic Montour County, on the point formed by the confluence of the north and west branches of the Susquehanna River, approximately 55 miles north of Harrisburg.

This is the original building; the present station was built in 1910 and has recently been converted to another use.

EASTON, PENNSYLVANIA

This comparatively recent structure, built in 1927, is now used as a signal tower by the Lehigh Valley Railroad. It is typical of most railroad signal towers with its concrete foundation and brick walls, and is topped by an asbestos-shingled wooden roof.

Photo by Pennsylvania Historical and Museum Commission, Harrisburg, Pennsylvania

EASTON, PENNSYLVANIA

The town of Easton, at the junction of the Lehigh and Delaware Rivers, has been a center of transportation since colonial times.

The present station was constructed in 1887 on a railroad line opened in 1867; it is not the original building. At one time the Easton station, on the main line between New York and Harrisburg, served the finest trains operating between New York and Chicago, including the Wagoner Palace cars. The depot is now unoccupied.

The stations at Easton, Bethlehem, Allentown, and Jim Thorpe were all painted by the artist when they were part of the Central Railroad of New Jersey, prior to their being acquired by the Lehigh Valley Railroad System in 1971.

BETHLEHEM, PENNSYLVANIA

The architectural style of the 1850's coupled with the French influence which produced the mansard roof, was highly acclaimed and enthusiastically received. The overhanging roof offered protection to passengers on the platform. Because it was supported by large brackets, it needed no pillars, and thus did not interfere with passengers boarding the train.

The station was built in 1873, and was once part of the Central Railroad of New Jersey. It served the most luxurious trains running from New York to Chicago. Now the station at Bethlehem is used only for freight shipments for the Lehigh & New England Railroad.

Since 1966 the Junior Chamber of Commerce has demonstrated its interest in this remarkable structure by restoring the exterior and completely modernizing the interior. High maintenance costs now threaten even the fine efforts of the JAYCEES; hopefully they will be able to raise additional funds to continue upkeep.

ALLENTOWN, PENNSYLVANIA

As part of the Central Railroad of New Jersey, this brick building once served such noted trains as the Scranton Flyer, the Queen of the Valley and the Harrisburg Special. The station dates back to 1903 and is presently used as a freight office.

ALLENTOWN, PENNSYLVANIA

The interlocking tower at the Union Street
Crossing was a box-like structure,
situated near the Auburn Street Crossing
tower. It was razed after the station it
served discontinued service.

Ranulph Bye

ALLENTOWN, PENNSYLVANIA

Actually more of an elevated watchman's shanty than a signal tower, this structure at the Auburn Street Crossing has been demolished since the artist painted it.

Similar towers are fast disappearing from the scene as the computer world, the great mechanics of our age, replace small watchman's shanties.

ALLENTOWN, PENNSYLVANIA

This elevated structure was the
watchman's shelter and gate control
house. It once was located near the
signal tower at the Auburn Street
crossing. It has since been demolished.

Ranulph Bye

ALLENTOWN, PENNSYLVANIA

For more than 60 years the famous Black Diamond Express made Allentown a regular stop on its run. So did the Wyoming Valley Express, the Wilkes-Barre Night Express, the Buffalo-Toronto Express and the Lehigh Limited!

This monolithic structure, built in 1890, was on the main line of the Lehigh Valley Railroad between New York and Buffalo. Its foundation was unique in that it was actually built into the East Hamilton Street bridge that crossed over its tracks. The station, abandoned in 1962, was sold with its surrounding land, probably for land development.

TOPTON, PENNSYLVANIA

Situated in a small town, 19 miles east of
Reading, the Topton depot is a one-story
brick structure.
  The depot, now on the Reading line,
was completed in 1874 for the North
Pennsylvania Railroad, which began
operations in 1869.

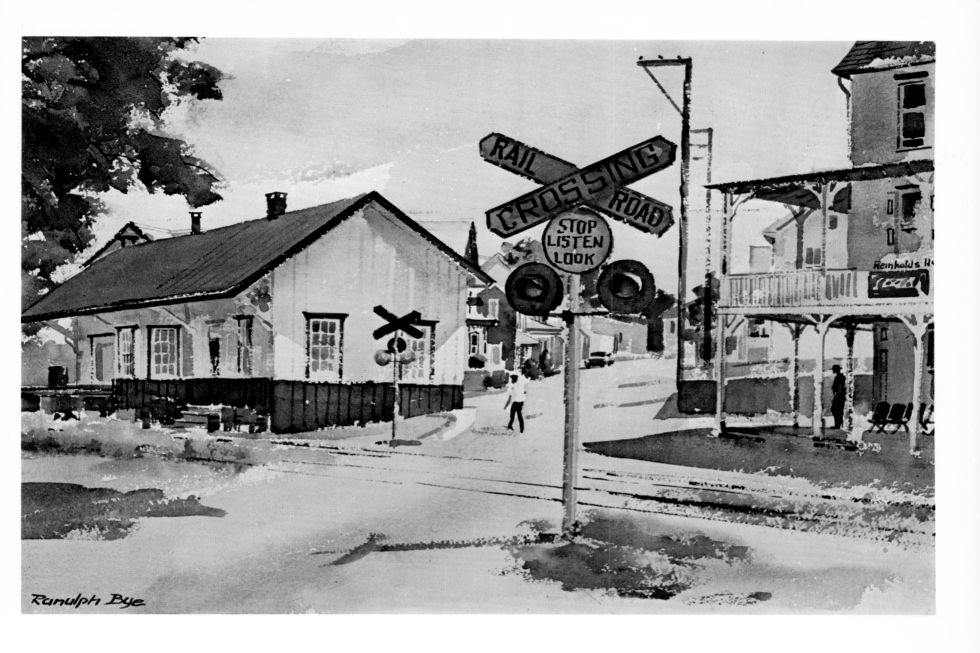

REINHOLDS, PENNSYLVANIA

Reinholds station was built in 1905 in the
heart of the Pennsylvania Dutch country,
13 miles west of Reading, and was on the
Lancaster branch of the Reading Railroad.
It is now being used by a commercial
plumbing and heating company. The
Reinholds Hotel is also pictured.

BIRDSBORO, PENNSYLVANIA

The Wilmington & Reading Division of
the Reading Company joins the main
stem of the Philadelphia & Reading at
Birdsboro.
 This frame structure, built about 1910,
has some unusual features, which include
a raised platform skirting the entire
building and a graceful arch spanning
the inside gable. The depot appeared to
be unused when painted by the artist on
April 16, 1973.

Ranulph Bye

SINKING SPRING, PENNSYLVANIA

The Lebanon Valley branch of the
Reading Company once served this
station, but passenger service has been
discontinued. Its one-story, irregularly-
shaped frame building with freight house
dates back to 1872. The railroad line
opened in 1859.

LEBANON, PENNSYLVANIA

Built in the 1880's and designed by the
estimable Stanford White, the station was
quite imposing with its terra cotta
ornamental embellishments on chimneys,
gables and cornices.

It was served by the 22-mile long
Cornwell & Lebanon Railroad which ran
on the Pennsylvania's main line east of
Harrisburg. The railroad has been out of
service since the flood of June, 1972.

GETTYSBURG, PENNSYLVANIA

In 1863 President Lincoln arrived by train to deliver his famous address. It was also the home station for President Eisenhower, the most distinguished resident of Gettysburg. Through the years it served a number of official trains, as well as many visitors to this historic site.

This is a beautiful station with an elegant cupola; still the original building on the original site. The station was built by the Gettysburg Railroad in 1858 on the old Hanover Junction and Gettysburg Line. It later became part of the Western Maryland Railroad system.

During the Civil War it was an important depot for evacuating the wounded from the battlefield. Today the station has been converted to the home of the Gettysburg Tourist Bureau.

Ranulph Bye

Collection of Division of Mechanical & Civil Engineering Museum of History and Technology, Smithsonian Institution

POINT OF ROCKS, MARYLAND

The present two-story brick station at
Point of Rocks, complete with Italianate
stonework and Bavarian bell tower, was
built in 1871.

There was a predecessor at this site,
opened by the Baltimore & Ohio line in
the early 1830's.

Ranulph Bye

YORK, PENNSYLVANIA

York station was built sometime between 1885 and 1895 as part of the Northern Central Railway Company. It was later leased by Penn Central.

In 1946 as many as 28 trains a day, destined for Chicago, Erie and Buffalo used the station. It is still associated with the old depot hotel across the street, which is still standing. Since April of 1973 the station itself is not in service as such.

ELLICOTT CITY, MARYLAND

This depot is another real old timer, built in 1831, unusually well-preserved despite its age. It was declared a National Historic Landmark in 1968.

Ellicott City prospered for awhile after the station was built, but went downhill. The town was rejuvenated when the Tom Thumb, a tiny woodburning "vertical boiler", made its historic maiden voyage on the nation's first railroad track, which was part of the Baltimore & Ohio Railroad. The route of the Tom Thumb was from Baltimore to Ellicott's Mill, approximately 13 miles away.

Ranulph Bye

LAUREL, MARYLAND

On the main line of the Baltimore &
Ohio Railroad, Laurel is about halfway
between Baltimore and Washington. The
station was built in 1903. Pittsburgh,
Chicago and St. Louis trains used the
tracks until 1957.

TAKOMA PARK, MARYLAND

Takoma Park, just north of our nation's
capitol, once was served by this station,
a stop on the Baltimore & Ohio line.
Built in 1893, the single-story frame
structure fell victim to fire a few years
ago.

ROCKVILLE, MARYLAND

This attractive two-story brick station at
Rockville is of Gothic design and dates
back to 1878. On the Baltimore & Ohio's
main line, the depot is approximately 12
miles northwest of Washington, D.C.

GAITHERSBURG, MARYLAND

Gaithersburg has a charming station which dates back to 1878. Of particular interest is the use of spools and spindles under the overhang, rather an unusual trim.

It is the next station after Rockville on the Baltimore & Ohio's Metropolitan Branch to Point of Rocks, Harpers Ferry and Cumberland; it is between Cumberland and Washington, D.C.

The station, with ticket office, is still used by commuters.

HARPERS FERRY, WEST VIRGINIA

This historic town, 55 miles northwest
of Washington, D.C., takes pride in its
two-story station, built in 1894.

Harpers Ferry was established as a
U.S. arsenal in 1796; it is famous as the
site of John Brown's raid in 1859, which
signaled the start of the Civil War. In the
war between the states, Harpers Ferry
was of strategic importance, situated as
it was at the lower end of the Shenandoah
Valley. The occupation of the arsenal
changed from Federal to Confederate
hands a number of times as the war
progressed. After the battle of Gettysburg,
it remained in Federal hands until the
cessation of hostilities in 1865.

The depot is now a National Parks
Service Historic Site, and passenger
service is still maintained.

Collection of John A. Meyer, Jr., Coach Inn, Ft. Washington, Pa.

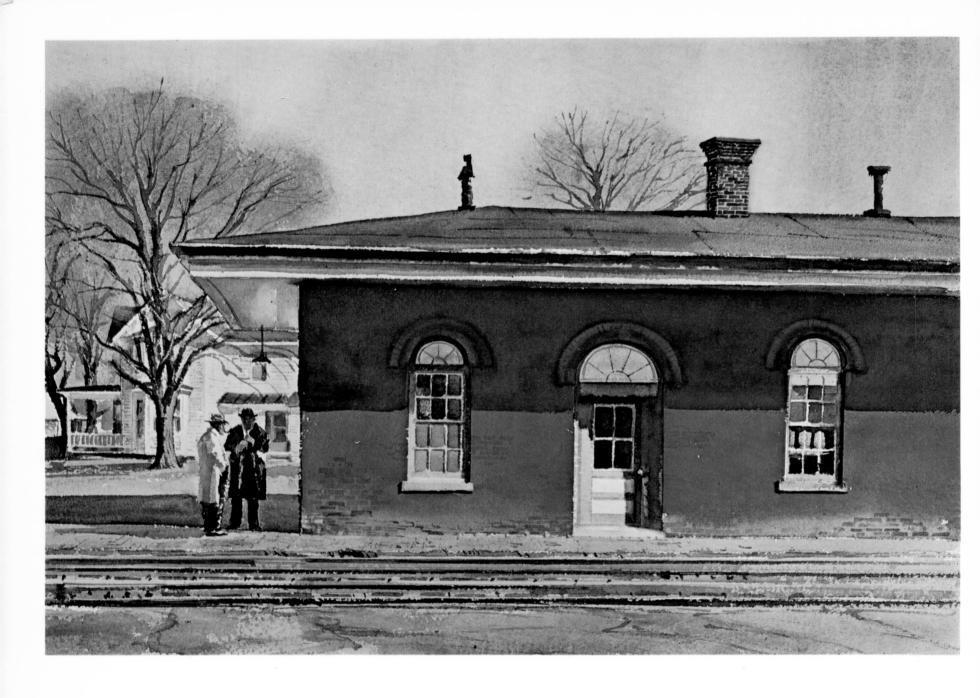

CLAYTON, DELAWARE

It must have been an exciting time for
Clayton when, in 1884, the Philadelphia
& Norfolk Railroad completed tracks for
its Delaware Division (later incorporated
into the Pennsylvania System).

This colorful station, with its
semicircular fanlight over the windows
and doorway, was ready to welcome
passengers. Clayton is about 37 miles
south of Wilmington.

HAMMONTON, NEW JERSEY

Sixty miles of railroad track were completed by the Camden & Atlantic Railroad in 1854. The train's route originated at Camden (Cooper's Ferry), with passenger pick-ups at Hammonton and Egg Harbor City. It terminated at Atlantic City.

The original depot was only a short distance from the present Bellevue Avenue location, established in 1858. Hammonton station later became part of the Pennsylvania-Reading Seashore Lines.

MT. HOLLY, NEW JERSEY

Mt. Holly station is no more. It used to be
a busy place, only 20 miles from
Philadelphia, including the ferry distance
across the Delaware River. The
Philadelphia & Long Branch Railroad
once had a stop there, later the
Pennsylvania line.

CHATSWORTH, NEW JERSEY

The Blue Comet once stopped here. The famous "flyer" was on the route of the Central Railway of New Jersey and stopped at Chatsworth, where the small frame depot had a chance to show off its scalloped-shingle siding.

Located in the heart of the Pine Barrens in south-central New Jersey, it has no passenger service today, but is used for the area's well-known crops of cranberries and blueberries, and lumber.

COSSART STATION, PENNSYLVANIA

Originally Cossart Station was an old dwelling built in 1895. Complete with a porch, this frame structure always looked more like a farmhouse than a depot.

Cossart Station is located in the Brandywine Valley, 13 miles north of Wilmington, Delaware. It was at one time on the Wilmington & Northern Railroad and was later leased to the Reading Railroad.

A two-story stone station and agents dwelling was built in 1929 to replace the frame depot. This stone structure now serves as an office and storage area for a farm.

GLEN MILLS, PENNSYLVANIA

Another from the 1880's, this station was
part of the Philadelphia & Baltimore, later
served by the Pennsylvania Railroad.
Constructed of brick, it has the fairly
common two stories, with ticket office
and living quarters.

It's situated about 20 miles southwest
of Philadelphia.

OVERBROOK, PHILADELPHIA
PENNSYLVANIA

This frame building has a large over-hanging roof to protect passengers on the platform. The station itself consists of a waiting room and ticket office; living quarters are attached.

Overbrook was a country station until 1890. It dates back to the 1870's and served a railroad line that had opened in 1849. It once had a proud bearing, but has been neglected of late.

The station is situated on the Philadelphia-Montgomery County boundary line, near City Line Avenue. The Penn Central carries many commuters to center city Philadelphia from this heavily-used depot.

FAIRMOUNT PARK, PHILADELPHIA, PENNSYLVANIA

On the Reading line, the quaint signal
tower was dwarfed when the Expressway,
towering overhead, was opened to traffic.
It was dismantled in 1966.

UPSAL, PHILADELPHIA PENNSYLVANIA

The depot is partially of brick, designed in the Victorian style known as "Gingerbread." On the Pennsy line, it goes back to approximately 1882. It is quite similar to the station at Strafford, but not as old.

Ranulph Bye

WISSAHICKON, PHILADELPHIA, PENNSYLVANIA

This freight station was built in 1892 on the Philadelphia-Reading Railroad, a line which opened in 1836. The passenger station appearing in the background is on its original site as well.

ALLEN LANE, PHILADELPHIA, PENNSYLVANIA

Although the station itself is not represented in this view, the lower level platform, protective walkways and overpass are shown.

Built in 1884, the depot is on the Chestnut Hill Branch of the Penn Central, formerly the Pennsylvania Railroad. Its design is typical of most on this line; waiting room and ticket office downstairs, living quarters above.

WAYNE, PENNSYLVANIA

Typical of present suburban stations
between Paoli and 30th Street Station,
Wayne is a Penn Central stop on the
commuter route to Philadelphia.

In the old days, between 1833 and
1857, the depot was on the Main Line
of Public Works, Philadelphia to
Pittsburgh. The Main Line of Public Works
was a system of railways and canals
linking Philadelphia with the Ohio River
ordered by the Pennsylvania Legislative
in 1828.

Ranulph Bye

BRYN MAWR, PENNSYLVANIA

Located on the main line of the Penn
Central, 10 miles from Penn Center
Station, this freight house was completed
sometime in the 1870's. Its roof has a
chopped gable, a type known as "jerkin'
head."

There was an adjacent depot but it was
torn down to make way for a small
utilitarian structure.

STRAFFORD, PENNSYLVANIA

This building was one of the attractions
at the Philadelphia Centennial; it was
used as the official catalog building.
After the exposition was over, the station
was moved to its present site on the Penn
Central's main line.

The depot has lost none of its charm
and is very well maintained, still used
by commuters.

STRAFFORD

Ranulph Bye

NORTH WALES, PENNSYLVANIA

The distinguishing feature of this station is the use of iron supports under the overhanging roof instead of wooden beams. The iron supports evidently were experimental, since this method was not used on later and similar stations.

Built in 1860 on a railroad line opened four years prior, the North Wales station was leased to the Reading Company in 1879. North Wales is 22 miles from Philadelphia on the main line to Bethlehem, Pennsylvania. The station is in active use.

MT. AIRY, PHILADELPHIA,
PENNSYLVANIA

This two-story frame passenger station
was completed in 1883 for the former
Philadelphia & Reading Railway. It cost
approximately $8,000.

On the Chestnut Hill branch of the
Reading, the station is a little over 9
miles from the company's terminal in
Philadelphia, and is widely used.

NEW BRITAIN, PENNSYLVANIA

Another diamond jubilee model, typical
of the country depots built just before
the turn of the century . . . frame
construction, single-story, with a peak
roof. It has an agent's office and waiting
room; the freight house is separate. It is
served by the Doylestown Branch of the
Reading Company, and is roughly 32
miles north of Philadelphia.

SELLERSVILLE, PENNSYLVANIA

Initially this was Sellers Tavern on the
Bethlehem Pike. The irregularly-shaped
brick structure, built in 1901, was
converted into a passenger station by the
North Pennsylvania Railroad, which had
been operating since 1857.

Ramulph Bye

Photo by Pennsylvania Historical and Museum Commission, Harrisburg, Pennsylvania

DOYLESTOWN, PENNSYLVANIA

The first major outlet to the great
outside world was in 1856, when a
branch of the North Pennsylvania
Railroad began service, uniting with the
main line at Lansdale, 10 miles away.
Until then, the stage coach was the link
between Doylestown and Philadelphia.

This substantial station, built in 1871,
is still very much in use, operated by the
Reading Company.

Ranulph Bye

PERKASIE, PENNSYLVANIA

Another one-story freight station representative of most of its time. Freight handling began in 1887.

The passenger station, which came four years later, can be seen in the background. Both facilities are still in existence, but only the freight office is operating.

WYCOMBE, PENNSYLVANIA

On June 19, 1891, plans for a depot were completed and construction was soon started. Until that time a passenger car was used as a combination ticket and freight office. A permanent installation was needed to accommodate the busy community, then known as Walton Station.

Ranulph Bye

NEW HOPE, PENNSYLVANIA

New Hope is one of the most charming of all the stations in this collection.

Victorian flair is the key word here. The station's features include its small, irregularly-shaped frame structure, colored windowpanes and Norman tower.

Quaint New Hope station has been moved twice in recent years and is presently at its original site. It was built in 1889 and was formerly served by the New Hope Branch of the Reading Company.

Purchased from the Reading in the 1960's by the New Hope & Ivyland, a common carrier railroad, the station at New Hope has become a famous local landmark. Now restored, it is home base for the steam train that delights young and old as it makes its 17-mile trip across historic Solebury and Buckingham Townships.

LAMBERTVILLE, NEW JERSEY

The original building, a frame structure, was replaced by the present station in 1874. The depot is noted for its massive size, large dormer windows and unusual cupola. Until 1906 it housed the general offices of the superintendent of the Belvedere-Delaware Railroad.

After the Civil War, Lambertville station was an important machine and repair shop for the Pennsylvania Railroad. (The old Belvedere-Delaware was purchased by the Pennsy in 1971).

The station is located on a narrow belt of land between the Delaware River and the Raritan Canal. It is now used only by the Railway Express Agency.

HOPEWELL, NEW JERSEY

The two-story brick building at Hopewell
is an excellent example of the mansardic
era, also known as the "General Grant"
style. It was built in 1882 for the
Delaware & Bound Brook Railroad.

The railroad line, opened in May, 1876,
was one of the carriers built for
excursionists from New York (via the
Central Railroad of New Jersey) to the
Philadelphia Centennial. The Philadelphia
& Reading acquired the original road in
1879.

The colorful and fascinating interior
of the ticket office is shown at right.

71

PENNINGTON, NEW JERSEY

This station is almost identical in design to the one at Hopewell, except that Pennington is a stone structure, not brick.

Completed in 1882, the station was built on a railroad line opened in May, 1876. It was originally served by the Delaware & Bound Brook Railroad and later leased by the Reading.

The Pennington depot is not in service, but its living quarters on the second floor are being used by a Reading Company agent and his family.

SKILLMAN, NEW JERSEY

Completed in 1879, the station is similar
to the one at Weston-Manville. This view
looking north shows the platform and
bay window of the agent's office as of
October, 1964, two years before the
station was razed.

MANVILLE-FIDERNE, NEW JERSEY

Built in 1878, the two-story frame depot
at Manville-Fiderne was a Central Railroad
of New Jersey stop between Plainfield
and Somerville. The road was operative
in 1841, and had extended tracks as far
as Phillipsburg by 1852. The depot was
torn down in the spring of 1972.

WESTON-MANVILLE, NEW JERSEY

Weston-Manville station was built in 1882
by the Philadelphia-Reading Railroad.
The original line, the Delaware & Bound
Brook, had begun service on the track in
May, 1876. It was a 27-mile line from
Bound Brook through Weston-Manville,
Hopewell and Pennington to West
Trenton, formerly Trenton Junction.

MILFORD, NEW JERSEY

This station now handles freight only. It is regrettable because it is located on one of the most scenic rail lines to be found anywhere. Originating at Trenton and following the upstream course of the Delaware River for over 60 miles, the Belvedere-Delaware then connected with the Lackawanna Railroad.

Completed in the 1880's, the station is of half stone, half timber construction.

Ranulph Bye

ELIZABETH, NEW JERSEY

The Elizabeth station is a stop on Penn Central's New York local, as well as a commuter station on the Central Railroad's route to points along the New Jersey shore.

The eastbound building shown here was built between 1891 and 1892. The lower portion is quarry-faced stone, the upper is yellow glazed brick. The clock at the top of the 76-foot tower has not succumbed to automation; it has to be wound by hand once a week.

FANWOOD-SCOTCH PLAINS, NEW JERSEY

The westbound station pictured here was built about 1868. This depot was part of the Central Railroad of New Jersey. It has been restored and is maintained by the local Junior Chamber of Commerce.

The overpass is of steel construction with timber. It was built in 1942 and remained an open walkway until a roof was added in 1948.

Ranulph Bye

JERSEY CITY TERMINAL, NEW JERSEY

This terminal at Jersey City is the third and final, built between 1913-15, out of deference to modernization and the need for expansion. Like its predecessors, it was both a train and ferry facility, a major commuter station to Manhattan.

The first structure was built in 1864, the second in 1890. Both outlived their ability to accommodate more tracks, bigger trains.

Commuters often had the company of celebrities and "big name" bands, because of available connections to and from the resort areas of New Jersey and Pennsylvania.

A detail of its clock tower is shown at right.

HACKENSACK, NEW JERSEY

The station at Anderson Street,
completed about 1890, was originally on
the New Jersey & New York Railroad,
later the Erie Railroad. It is 14½ miles
from Jersey City and still in service.

In order to complete more fully the
composition, the Victorian house to the
right of the station was added and the
signal tower on the extreme right moved.

LYNDHURST, NEW JERSEY

On the Delaware, Lackawanna & Western
Railroad, the depot was built on high
foundations in order to match the height
of the tract.

The westbound depot had the station
area level with the track; living quarters
were below.

The station was completed in 1883,
gone in 1972.

GREAT MEADOWS, NEW JERSEY

This station was completed in 1883 at an
approximate cost of $3,000. It was used
by the Federal Express between Boston
and Washington until 1917, and was then
served by the Lehigh & Hudson River
Railroad Company. Now the depot is
used for freight only, since passenger
service was discontinued in 1939.

TENAFLY, NEW JERSEY

The painting to the right shows the most notable feature of the Tenafly station— the distinctive green cupola topped by a hand-wrought weathervane.

Many similar stations outside the cities of New York, Boston and Philadelphia were ornately designed. This was indicative of the affluent communities in which they were located.

Tenafly station was built in 1880 by the Northern Railroad of New Jersey; it was acquired by the town of Tenafly in 1963.

DEMAREST, NEW JERSEY

The steeple on this depot distinguishes
it from the average commuter station.
Built in 1869 of stone, it was once part
of the Erie Railroad system, and is still
in existence though out of service.

HILLSDALE, NEW JERSEY

Originally served by the New Jersey &
New York Railroad and later by the Erie,
the station at Hillsdale is of frame
construction with a slate roof. It was
built in 1878. Hillsdale is about 22 miles
north of Jersey City.

Photo by Pennsylvania Historical and Museum Commission, Harrisburg, Pennsylvania

BRONX, NEW YORK

Located at 174th Street and Hoe Avenue, the elevated station illustrated has all the manifestations of the Victorian era . . . colorful glass, wood and iron ornamentation.

The concept of the elevated railway was a marvel of its time and a tremendous engineering feat. It provided the maximum utilization of space, while allowing for pedestrian and auto traffic below, a rapid, mass transit system above.

SPARKILL, NEW YORK

In 1844 the first woodburning train began operating; in 1959 the first train departed Sparkill to Jersey City.

The station illustrated was built in 1878; once served by the Northern Railroad of New Jersey, later by the Erie-Lackawanna.

The town of Sparkill acquired the depot in the mid-1960's but had it razed in 1972.

PEEKSKILL, NEW YORK

Built in 1896 for the New York Central
Railroad, the station at Peekskill is gone,
another victim of time.
    During the railroad era the downtown
hotel across the street from the station
was as much a part of the scene as the
depot itself.

KINGSTON, NEW YORK

This lovely old town is 90 miles northwest of New York City. The former station, torn down in 1964, was probably laid out as a combination depot-hotel complete with dining room. Completed in the late 1860's, it was on the defunct New York, Ontario & Western Railroad.

WURTSBORO, NEW YORK

Located 26 miles northeast of Port Jervis
on the Port Jervis & Kingston Division,
the one-story frame building at Wurtsboro
is part of the New York, Ontario &
Western Railroad which was abandoned
about 1957. It is still standing.

Ranulph Bye

OLD SAYBROOK, CONNECTICUT

This large frame structure, built in 1873, is typical of the frame buildings of the New Haven Railroad (later incorporated into the Penn Central).

The depot is still in use, with a ticket agent on duty to serve travelers to New York, 96 miles away.

STAMFORD, CONNECTICUT

The signal tower at Stamford is typical of the many signal towers along the main line of the New Haven Railroad.

CANAAN, CONNECTICUT

At one time Canaan was the busy junction and crossing of the New York, New Haven & Hartford and the Central New England Railroads. The station itself dates back to 1872. In the early 1900's, 16 trains of the New Haven and 20 trains of the Central New England stopped here.

The destination of the New Haven line was the Berkshires; the Central New England ran from Hartford to Poughkeepsie.

Ranulph Bye

WATERBURY, CONNECTICUT

The construction date for the Waterbury
station was in 1909. With its very high
clock tower it is a near replica of the
Palazzo Vecchio in Florence, Italy.

The station is now used as the offices
of a newspaper since discontinuance of
service by the Penn Central.

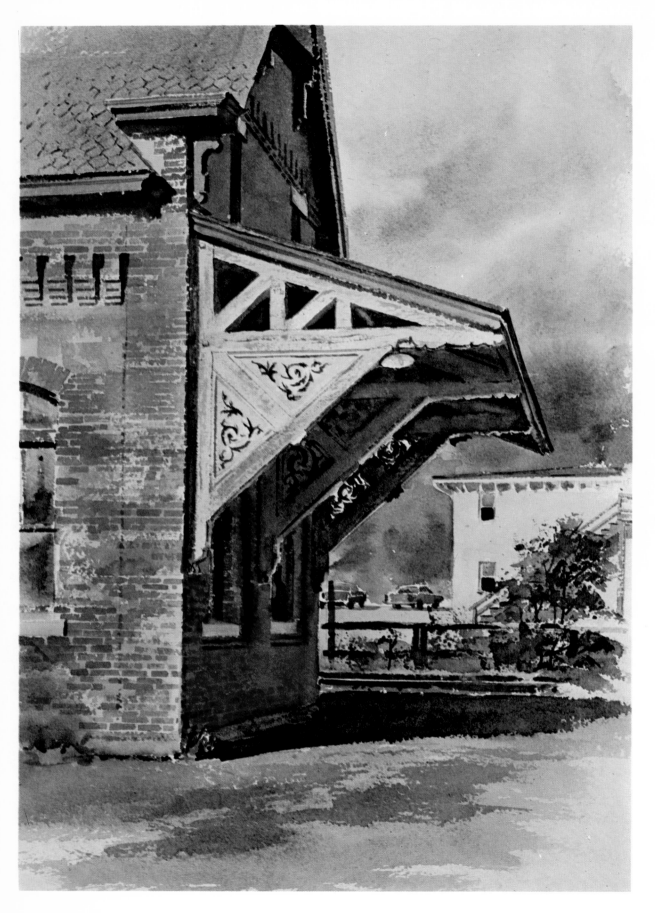

THOMASTON, CONNECTICUT

This architectural detail of the Thomaston station shows the overhanging roof and intricately designed brackets. The station is still extant.

COS COB, CONNECTICUT

A simple frame structure, still in service, it is representative of many of the stations along the main line of the New Haven Railroad between New York and Boston. It was built sometime between 1880 and 1910, and is located near the Connecticut-New York State boundary.

PEACEDALE, RHODE ISLAND

The Narraganset Pier Railroad, founded
in 1872, served this station.
Note the interesting bracket treatment
over the door and bay windows of the
two-story structure. Both the railroad and
the depot were recently purchased by a
dentist who is also a railroad buff, and
he and his family live on the second floor
of the station. His plans are to begin
excursion trips three days a week; the
train will run between Peacedale and
Narraganset Pier.

BUZZARDS BAY, MASSACHUSETTS

The station at Buzzards Bay, built in 1913, was part of the New Haven Railroad, later on the Penn Central system.

The white depot, with its brick and stucco construction, tile roof and floor, evokes a definite Spanish flavor. Another noteworthy feature, indicative of the engineering skill of the time, is the drawbridge behind the station which crosses the Cape Cod Canal.

CHATHAM, MASSACHUSETTS

The station was completed in 1887.
Service to Chatham was started by the
Chatham Railroad, which later became
part of the New Haven Railroad system.

The well-preserved building with its
finely proportioned octagonal tower and
roof of "feather-tipped" shingles is now
a railroad museum, having been restored
by the town of Chatham.

Ranulph Bye

WHITMAN, MASSACHUSETTS

The New York, New Haven & Hartford
Railroad once served this depot. Whitman
is located 21 miles from South Station,
Boston. The station was destroyed by
fire in the summer of 1972.

MIDDLEBURY, VERMONT

This station is on the defunct Rutland
Railway, over which trains such as the
Green Mountain Flyer once sped between
New York and Montreal.

Contracts disposing of stations to
private businesses usually contain an
extra clause which stipulates that the
buyer must move the building away from
the railroad's right-of-way. The station,
now an auto parts supply store, is on
the same site, since the clause was
omitted in the purchase agreement.

CRAWFORD NOTCH, NEW HAMPSHIRE

Located in the heart of the White
Mountains, the Crawford Notch station is
85 miles northwest of Portland, Maine.
Now closed, this station was once served
by the Maine Central Railroad, which
later became the Boston & Maine.

The Crawford House, which dates back
to the 1870's, can be seen in the
background; it is still a flourishing hotel.

NORTH CONWAY, NEW HAMPSHIRE

Located at the southern entrance to the
White Mountains region, North Conway is
137 miles north of Boston.

This imposing station was completed in
1872, and was served by the Boston &
Maine Railroad. It was designed to
conform with the opulent resort hotels
built during the latter half of the 19th
century. It is, today, a prototype of the
railroad station of its time, and is to be
restored and used as the depot for a
steam railroad, a tourist attraction.

Ranulph Bye